I can get fit!

Written by Clare Helen Welsh

Illustrated by Ángeles Peinador

Collins

Mum huffs and huffs.

Mum kicks to get fit.

Bud runs and runs.

Bud runs to get fit.

Deb hops and bobs.

Deb hops to get fit.

Nan puffs and puffs.

Nan sits to get fit.

Can I get fit?

beds

I dig in the beds.

I puff if I dig.

I dig to get fit.

/b/

14

 After reading

Letters and Sounds: Phase 2

Word count: 56

Focus phonemes: /g/ /o/ /c/ /k/ ck /e/ /u/ /r/ /h/ /b/ /f/ ff

Common exception words: and, to, I, the

Curriculum links: Physical development; Understanding the world

Early learning goals: Reading: read and understand simple sentences; use phonic knowledge to decode regular words and read them aloud accurately; read some irregular words

Developing fluency

- Your child may enjoy hearing you read the book.
- Encourage your child to read the text, emphasising the verbs, such as **runs**, **hops**, **puffs**. Point out the question mark on page 10 and demonstrate reading the words in a questioning tone.

Phonic practice

- Point to the word **huffs** on page 2. Ask your child to sound out and then blend the word. (*h/u/ff/s* – **huffs**) Talk about how the two letters "ff" make one sound /f/.
- On page 8, ask your child to find, sound out and blend another word with a similar spelling. (*p/u/ff/s* – **puffs**)
- On page 3, point to **kicks**. Ask your child to sound out and then blend the word. (*k/i/ck/s* – **kicks**) Ask: Which two different letters together make the /c/ sound? (*ck*)
- Look at the "I spy sounds" pages (14 and 15). Point to the bike and say: I spy /b/ in bike. Challenge your child to point to and name different things they can see containing a /b/ sound. (e.g. *ball, blue bat, burgers, bench, bread buns, basket, barbecue, bottle, butterfly, butter, bananas, bowl, Bud*)

Extending vocabulary

- Talk about the meaning of **huff** and **puff**. (e.g. *breathe hard/get out of breath from doing something with your body, like running*) Challenge your child to think of as many activities as they can that make people huff or puff. Encourage them to think of things we do at home (e.g. *walking upstairs, digging the garden*) and things that we do outside, such as sports. (e.g. *swimming, football, tennis*)